# THE EMMAUS MODEL

*Discipleship, Theological Education, and Transformation*

# THE EMMAUS MODEL

*Discipleship, Theological Education, and Transformation*

Bruce G. Allder and David A. Ackerman

*Global Nazarene Publications*

ISBN 978-1-56344-912-3
rev2019-11-19

Published by
Global Nazarene Publication   &   Asia-Pacific Region
Lenexa, Kansas (USA)              Church of the Nazarene

Copyright © 2019
Bruce G. Allder and David A. Ackerman

DIGITAL PRINTING

All rights reserved. No part of this publication may be reproduced, stored in a retrieval system, or transmitted in any form or by any means—for example, electronic, photocopy, recording—without the prior written permission of the publisher. The only exception is brief quotations in printed reviews.

Scripture quotations marked NIV are from the Holy Bible, New International Version. Copyright © 1973, 1978, 1984, 2011 by the International Bible Society. Used by permission of Zondervan Publishing House. All rights reserved.

Scripture quotations marked NKJV are from the New King James Version. Copyright © 1982 by Thomas Nelson. Used by permission. All rights reserved.

# TABLE OF CONTENTS

Forward .................................................................. 6

Introduction ............................................................ 7

Chapter 1: Our Mission of Disciple Making ........................... 11

Chapter 2: Education in the Nazarene Perspective ................. 20

Chapter 3: Transition of Models ...................................... 34

Chapter 4: The Emmaus Journey ..................................... 43

Chapter 5: Implementing the Model ................................. 50

Conclusion ............................................................. 62

Bibliography ........................................................... 65

# FORWARD

The mission of the Church of the Nazarene is "To Make Christlike Disciples in the Nations". Old paradigms and practices are changing. The church is growing rapidly in some world areas, often with a lack of sufficiently trained leaders to insure orthodoxy and coherency. To be more effective in this mission to which God calls us, this book provides a practical way whereby we can rethink our models and methods of education and ministerial preparation for the purpose of equipping God's people for works of service that his body might be built up.

The vision and methodology shared in this book is that of an integrated educational system centered in reflective practice that engages everyone; from the person who is exploring faith in the local church, to the one seeking higher education through an educational institution. The Emmaus model as presented, introduces a new ethos of teaching as part of the discipleship process and of discipling as part of the educational process. It concisely and clearly brings together the concepts of mission and formation of Christlike character within community as the focus of theological education. Robert Banks affirms that when this is done properly, that "theological education is not a higher stage of Christian education, but a dimension of everyone's Christian education, depending upon their stage in life and calling." The Emmaus Model is about learning as we journey in community on the mission of God.

My prayer is that this book will form the foundation upon which all future discipleship and educational strategies are developed.

—Mark Louw, Regional Director
Asia-Pacific Church of the Nazarene

# INTRODUCTION

Jesus gave the mission to his followers of going into the world, preaching the good news, and making disciples of all nations (Matthew 28:19-20; Mark 16:15; Luke 24:48; John 20:21; Acts 1:8). The Church of the Nazarene embraces this mission of *making Christlike disciples in the nations*. The Church of the Nazarene around the world works to carry out this mission in all of its ministries. Theological education is one essential way to make disciples. Jesus told his disciples to "teach" people all that he commanded. Teaching is more than sitting in a classroom but any means by which people come to know the good news of Jesus and grow in relationship with him. As we learn, our commitment to Jesus is strengthened and it provides the way to help others on the journey of transformation.

There are many ways to teach people what Jesus taught. The church has traditionally emphasized the training of its clergy. No doubt this is important because an organization will only grow as strong as its leaders. However, he did not assign only clergy to be the ones to make disciples. Instead, the Great Commission of making disciples is for all believers. Therefore, the church must develop strategies for training people at all levels. This book offers a way of doing just that.

Nazarene higher education faces many new opportunities and challenges around the world. Old paradigms and methods are proving inadequate to reach a rapidly changing world. Theological education is part of this change. For several centuries, the predominant mode of theological education was for students to sit in classrooms and listen to lectures. Although there is value in this time-tested method, the changing learning environment demands creative rethinking of our educational methods. For example, the rise of technology has significantly changed the ability to access information. What used to be found only in libraries or from experts can now be accessed on a cell phone. Those born after 1990 have had access to technology that previous generations could not even imagine. The majority of the world now has access to mobile technology or the internet.

The shifting global landscape creates challenges for the church. The church is growing rapidly in some areas of the world, often resulting in a lack of trained leaders to insure orthodoxy and coherence. New emphases in experiential learning is forcing education to move outside the classroom. The number of adult learners who cannot attend a traditional college because of jobs, families, and distance has increased. This has necessitated a rethinking of theological education by extension. Learning has moved outside the classroom where students listen to lectures to active learning through new experiences. Educators are recognizing that learning involves more than simply receiving content but involves being shaped by new insights and changing attitudes and worldviews. The significant increase in travel and migration has brought the world to us through internationalization. Most cities of the world are now multi-cultural. The church is challenged with the rise of mega cities where the vast majority of residents are not-yet-believers. The world is now labeled as VUCA: **V**olatile, **U**ncertain, **C**omplex, and **A**mbiguous. How can we disciple people with all these challenges? How can we rethink education to meet Jesus' call to make disciples in this ever-changing world?

These new challenges require new methods. This book begins by looking at the reason for theological education. We must know the "why" before we explore the "what" or the "how." The authors are convinced that God is doing something new in, through, and even outside the church. The same Creator who spoke the universe into existence is stirring new and creative ideas in order to reach the world of today with the Good News of Jesus Christ. This book represents a new optimism fueled by Spirit-led imagination. God is doing a new movement around the world.

The purpose of this book is to equip disciple makers (disciplers) and educators from the local church through to the academy in carrying out the mission of Christ. This book has grown out of a conversation about how to "re-envision" theological education. Asia-Pacific Regional Director, Mark Louw, called together a group of experienced educators and practitioners to explore the challenges facing theological education on the region. The discussion explored the changes happening in education today and the need to train people for ministry in this shifting environment. The driving force of this conversation is the crucial need of character formation into Christlikeness during the educational process. Teaching knowledge alone will not win the world. The witness of lives transformed in Christ through the Holy Spirit will be the resource God uses to reach the world. The re-envisioning group hopes the ideas generated from the dialogue will be a catalyst for more innovative and effective strategies in theological education in Asia-Pacific and beyond.

This book represents a collective effort to explain this "why" and to show a way it can be carried out. David Ackerman, educational coordinator for the Philippines and Micronesia Church of the Nazarene, helped convene the conversation of the re-envisioning group. Bruce Allder, Senior Lecturer at Nazarene Theological College, Brisbane, Australia, developed a synthesis of models that provides a framework for effective theological education.

## THE EMMAUS MODEL

The new model is based on his reflection on the story of the risen Jesus appearing to two disciples on the road to Emmaus found in Luke 24:13-48. This book brings the ideas generated from the group's discussion and Allder's ideas together.

We hope this book unleashes the church of all ages and educational levels to develop leaders who are mission focused and equipped to make disciples who are then equipped to carry on the mission of multiplying more disciples.

# CHAPTER ONE

# Mission of Disciple Making

Jesus stated the mission of the church known as the "Great Commission" in Matthew 28:19-20:

> Therefore go and make disciples of all nations, baptizing them in the name of the Father and of the Son and of the Holy Spirit, and teaching them to obey everything I have commanded you. And surely I am with you always, to the very end of the age.

Jesus' plan for his followers became a reality with the coming of the Holy Spirit on the Day of Pentecost (Acts 1:8). After the filling of the Holy Spirit, the disciples moved from being "fishermen" in their boats to being engaged with the world as "fishers of people" (Matthew 4:19). Without the filling of the Holy Spirit, we cannot fulfil the mission Jesus gave us.

Our theology shapes what we do. The link between theology and outcome is crucial. Our theology informs our education which shapes what and how we teach which then determines what is produced. If our theology is sound, then we must explore our educational methods to determine their effectiveness in reaching the outcome of new disciples. If disciples are not being formed and multiplied as the outcome of our educational systems, then we must work our way backwards in this sequence to see what needs to be adjusted.

THEOLOGY → EDUCATION → DISCIPLE MAKING

## The Call to Love

The Great Commission gives us the "what" to do: make Christlike disciples. The Great Commandment gives us the "way" to do it: through relationships of love.

> Jesus said, "Love the Lord your God with all your heart and with all your soul and with all your mind." This is the first and greatest commandment. And the second is like it: "Love your neighbor as yourself." (Matthew 22:37-39)

The call to make disciples is rooted in the very character of God as loving and holy. God loves all people and wants all to experience salvation through Jesus Christ (John 3:16). Jesus told his disciples, "As the Father has sent me, I am sending you" (John 20:21). The call to make disciples is the call to know God in love and experience God's love for the world through the Holy Spirit. Theologians describe this as the *missio Dei*, the mission of God. The challenge for the church is how to be this loving community in mission. The church carries out this mission by serving as God's instrument of reconciliation and redemption in the likeness of Jesus Christ.

Stéphane Tibi, Educational Coordinator for the Eurasia Region and participant in the re-envisioning discussion, points out that in the Old Testament, two Hebrew words for *knowing* suggest different ways people learn. Both words are conveniently found in Proverbs 3:5-6:

> Trust in the Lord with all your heart,
> and lean not on your own **understanding** [*binah*].
> In all your ways **acknowledge** [*yada'*] him,
> and he will direct your paths. (NKJV)

According to Tibi, *binah* knowledge is analytical and scientific. It involves a subject that acts and an object that gives little feedback. This type of knowledge is not communication between the subject and the object. The information flows in only one direction: learning comes through observation of the data. *Yada'* knowledge, however, is personal and relational. It involves two-way communication. *Yada'* knowledge involves *binah*; data is important but only serves the greater purpose of relationship. It is difficult to develop relationship with only *binah*. When applied to the learning process, experiential knowledge (*yada'*) comes from the interaction and relationship built between teacher and student. *Yada'* fits well with making disciples by nurturing relationship with God and with neighbor. Learning takes place best in relationship, not simply with the accumulation of information.

The early church experienced growth through *yada'* type knowledge as believers developed in their relationship with God, one another, and those who did not believe yet. Their knowledge was an aspect of their love for God and love for others. According to Acts 2:42, four key practices helped these early believers in their mission: studying the apostles' teaching, fellowship with one another, sharing meals, and praying together. It is significant that these four processes all involved the community of faith. This community was filled with the Holy Spirit and had a vision to reach the world. They were stronger in love and prayer and deeper in their understanding of the gospel. This was a powerful combination for effective mission.

At the heart of theological education is growing deeper in our relationship with God through spiritual formation, in understanding ourselves through character development, and in knowledge about the world through awareness of context. This formation is a partnership of individuals responding to the Holy Spirit and other people in mutual support, dialogue, and accountability. The Holy Spirit is with us disciples as we journey through life together. Jesus as the Incarnate One fulfilled God's mission for him by living and identifying with humanity. He provides a model for how we can participate in God's mission. Theological education is more about transformation than information. At its core, it is participation in the mission of God. It begins with renewing the mind through the truth of the gospel (Romans 12:1-2). It includes change in character and every other part of life. It both shapes the mind and transforms the heart. The result is participation in what God is doing in the world now.

As we re-think discipleship and education, we must recognize that the call to make disciples is the universal call for all believers. This call should guide all we do in theological education. Within this universal call may be found specialized calls to leadership responsibilities within the church. Paul the Apostle wrote to the Ephesian church about this:

> So Christ himself gave the apostles, the prophets, the evangelists, the pastors and teachers, to equip his people for works of service, so that the body of Christ may be built up until we all reach unity in the faith and in the knowledge of the Son of God and become mature, attaining to the whole measure of the fullness of Christ (Ephesians 4:11-13).

As the body of Christ, the people of God are called to serve others and represent Christ to the world (John 20:21; Acts 1:8). Those with specialized calls of leadership help the church develop in its faith and knowledge of Christ. This necessitates both *binah* and *yada'* type knowledge. We must know the facts of Christ's teaching through studying the Bible and the story of God's people. But we must further respond by letting these facts penetrate our hearts so that our faith is more strongly rooted in Christ. As a result, the church will be "mature, attaining to the whole measure of the fullness of Christ" in its mission to the world (Eph 4:13). We can be better prepared to engage in this mission by being grounded in the knowledge of Christ and empowered by the Holy Spirit.

The church has a two-part responsibility in this process. First, as missional people, focused on the mission of becoming like Christ, we must go into the world with the hope of the gospel. Rather than feeling intimidated by the huge task before us, we can approach the mission with conviction that comes from knowing the good news (1 Peter 3:15). All believers can be trained to be disciple makers because God has given them gifts and what they need for this mission. Second, the church at all levels must develop an environment where people can hear the call of God to specialized ministries. With a strong vision for the world, the church as the Body of Christ becomes internally stronger. A church that nurtures its people in discipleship will be open to the movement of the Holy Spirit who will call people to specialized ministries to fulfill the mission of engaging the world.

Theological education that brings transformation will lead to more effective training of laity and clergy for this mission. It is a task for the whole church and not a select few professional clergy. Students learn to listen to God as they learn together in community. The Holy Spirit as the Counselor (John 14:26) sets the model for teachers to "come along side of" students. Mentors guide students through dialogue, encouragement, modeling, and accountability to grow into Christlikeness. Although this is a life-long journey, there can be markers along the way that indicate effectiveness in the mission.

## Discipleship and Education

This way of thinking about education challenges how the church has traditionally done discipleship. For over a thousand years, the church primarily followed the "parish model," which involves people coming to a central building (such as a cathedral or chapel) to learn about the gospel from trained clergy. The Protestant Reformation engrained this further with its emphasis on listening to sermons on Sunday mornings from pastors. Today, much of the church continues to follow this pattern. One of the unfortunate outcomes of this approach in Christian tradition has been to limit the "work force" of the church to only the 2% of Christians who are educated and ordained as members of the clergy. The other 98% are "fed" by the education of these few clergy.

This model of discipleship has also been reinforced and influenced by our theological education. Pastors are taught how to administer the parish and its associated mechanisms. The unfortunate result seen in the last two hundred years is a growing distance between the local church with its mission and the academy with its theologians. The challenge is to bring these together so that the church and academy work together to make disciples. Both the local church and the educational institution have vital roles to play in the task Jesus has given us.

The Board of General Superintendents of the Church of the Nazarene recognized the need to re-imagine the church amidst the changing contexts of today. The following description offers educators at all levels the opportunity to bring theological training to where people live. The "church" does not need to be held in a central building but wherever the people of God meet.

Any group that meets regularly for spiritual nurture, worship, or instruction at an announced time and place, with an identified leader, and aligned with the message and mission of the Church of the Nazarene can be recognized as a church and reported as such for district and general church statistics.

Theological education has a vital role in the disciple-making process. If the purpose of theological education is to equip and make effective "discipled disciplers," making Christlike disciples is not an optional elective in the curriculum but the essential outflow of faith leading to obedient action. Holiness is at the heart of this re-creation. Holiness leads to mission; mission requires education; education brings transformation. Methods of disciple making may change but the message and mission remain the same.

Five essential questions keep our mission focused in the right direction:

1. *What am I doing here?*—This is a question of **purpose**. Disciples of Christ are called by God and invited into God's mission in the world. We must live lives of purpose, which includes being discipled and discipling others.
2. *What is in my hand?*—This is a question of **passion**. God has given each person specific talents, desires, and gifts. This makes each of us unique! We shouldn't try to minister the exact same way others do; we should trust God's leading and design and find ways that uniquely fit us.
3. *Who is in front of me?*—This is a question focused on **people**. We are always interacting with others, and we should be intentional about loving people to Christ. This

requires that we take notice of people, value people, and follow the Lord's leading about when and how to share Christ with them.

4. *Do I know God's presence is with me?*—This is a question of **power**. Not our power but God's power within us through the Holy Spirit. We must be confident about who we are in God and aware of his leading in us. We must also recognize that we bring God's presence and power with us into the world and should move forward in boldness and confidence.

5. *What if everyone discipled the way I do?*—This is a question of **perspective**. This question is not meant to bring shame or guilt. Instead, it is meant to provide us with perspective and challenge us to live in God's purpose, based on our passion, focused on people, and guided by God's power. Remember, God wants to change the world through us, the church, the Body of Christ.

Theological education fulfills its purpose when students fulfill Jesus' commands. The outcome should be experiencing God's power through being equipped to bring others along on this transforming journey of re-creation. Through the work of the Holy Spirit, we can experience full and new life in Jesus Christ (2 Corinthians 3:18; 5:17). This new creation will be characterized by total dependence upon God, un-compromising compassion for humanity, deep knowledge of God's word, active love for the marginalized, empowered victory over temptation and sin, and effectiveness in preparing disciples who can continue the mission.

An important question to ask is, who are we educating? Are we simply preparing members of the clergy who acquire the professional skills of ministry? Or, are we engaged in an educational process that involves all people at all levels? God can use all people for his mission in whatever their profession or location in life. *Every occupation is an opportunity God uses to reach humanity.* People fail at this mission for two primary reasons: ignorance or sin. The first can lead to the second. The holiness message of transformation in Jesus Christ is the key to effectiveness in fulfilling the Great Commission.

To carry out this mission will require a refocusing of curriculum. Training disciple makers will require a balanced synthesis of being, doing, and knowing. If any of these three is left out or neglected, discipleship cannot happen. A disciple is someone who has responded to the call of Jesus to new life. "Being" places our identity with Jesus. We are connected to him in intimate relationship and learn to listen to our Master and Teacher. "Doing" is the mark of obedient love that comes as a response of faith in Jesus. Action is the response to listening and cannot be separated from relationship (see John 15:1). "Knowing" is the development of wisdom in response to worship and the study of the teachings of Jesus. We develop the "mind of Christ" as we get to know him more. The Great Commission ends with the significant words of relationship: "And surely I am with you always, to the very end of the age" (Matthew 28:20). Any model of education that seeks to be effective in our world today will require a close connection between heart formation ("being"), intellectual rigor ("knowing"), and effective action ("doing").

# CHAPTER TWO

# Education in the Nazarene Perspective

## Our Heritage of Being, Knowing, and Doing

Quality education has always been part of Nazarene DNA. This medical image describes one of the *Core Values* of the Church of the Nazarene related to our mission:

> We are a sent people, responding to the call of Christ and empowered by the Holy Spirit to go into all the world, witnessing to the Lordship of Christ and participating with God in the building of the Church and the extension of His kingdom (Matthew 28:19-20; 2 Corinthians 6:1). Our mission (a) begins in worship, (b) ministers to the world in evangelism and compassion, (c) encourages believers toward Christian maturity through discipleship, and (d) *prepares women and men for Christian service through Christian higher education.* (*Nazarene Essentials,* italics added).

Missionaries and denominational leaders recognized the connection between education and discipleship. Many of the denomination's educational institutions were founded soon after churches were planted in an area. This rich heritage provides a strong foundation upon which to build future innovations.

Nazarene education has most often focused on the "teach reteach" model in seeking to multiply churches and leaders in fulfillment of the Great Commission. Leaders are developed and taught how to multiply the work of discipleship by reteaching what they have learned. However, developing leaders based solely on the accumulation of knowledge is inadequate. Instead, the whole person must undergo change and growth into Christlikeness. This is why the Church of the Nazarene adopted the "4C's Model" for pastoral formation. It requires that our educational preparations stress *content*, *competency*, *character*, and *context* throughout the entire program.

Innovation continues around the world as the church seeks to meet the need for quality and visionary leaders. The church has shaped higher education and higher education has shaped the church. Our theology has impacted learning theory. Nazarene education is rooted in and guided by an optimistic view of God's grace and its ability to change people. We seek to put this optimism into practice through intentional, mission-focused engagement with the world, rather than retreating from it into the academy.

## The Development of Effective Strategies

In the 1990's, the Church of the Nazarene began to experience explosive growth in some parts of the world. Educational institutions were not able to keep up with the need for trained clergy and lay leaders. At that time, Robert Woodruff worked with the Nazarene World Mission Department to create a strategy to meet this need. The result was a booklet called, *Education on Purpose: Models for Education in World Areas*. Out of his efforts and through discussions, the hub and extension model developed. From this, our existing institutions and program were encouraged to become hubs that provided de-centralized theological training across districts and fields. Eventually, over 17,000 new pastors were trained in this manner.

THE EMMAUS MODEL

**Figure 1:** Focus in Education is an adaptation of Woodruff's "Focus in Education: Balanced Throughputs 4C's" (Woodruff, 29)

As Woodruff explains, the lens in his model (figure 1) provides the educational focus and purpose. The purpose will lead to intended outcomes. The purpose provides outcomes toward the focus. It is important to note that the creation of the program balances the 4C's. These provide the broad spectrum for developing students in being, knowing, and doing. Each of the 4C's contributes to the overall purpose of the course, program, or degree. Whatever this lens is will determine the outcomes that result. Everything is determined by the focus. The focus is the organizing principle for all aspects of a program. If the focus is not clear, everything else will be off balance.

There may be multiple possible focuses in education: the acquisition of knowledge and theory, development of practical skills, or spiritual formation. Each may require more or less input from each of the content, context, competency, and character inputs. If one of these is emphasized to the neglect of the others, the focus may not be as clear, the intended outcomes not met, or the focal point of the education not accomplished. Different courses and programs may have different focuses, but the input must still be balanced to achieve the intended outcomes.

With the possibility of multiple focuses to meet different situations, a robust model must be developed that integrates the balance of being, knowing, and doing with the mission that Jesus gave the church. In the broad terms emphasized in this booklet, the mission of disciple making must be somehow integrated into each educational program. Our proposal is that the primary focus of education in the Church of the Nazarene ought to match our broad mission of making Christlike disciples in the nations. This broad focus can be diversified and narrowed to meet the mission of a particular institution or ministry context, but somehow, it should still contribute to the goal of making disciples.

## Joining Discipleship and Education

The world is changing on numerous levels, yet our all-creative God is also doing new things as the revival winds of the Holy Spirit sweep the globe. Refocusing our purpose and retooling our methods will help us find our place in what God is doing. Educators now stress outcomes-based education. Everything we do in our education must help students accomplish specific outcomes. What are those outcomes? The list can be long, but they all must flow out of our desire to see our students become more Christlike and better equipped to participate in the mission of God. Education must lead to effective discipleship in fulfillment of the Great Commission. The journey of discipleship can happen as Christians intersect with those around them who have not yet put their faith in Jesus. In fulfillment of Jesus' command, disciples must be involved in the "teaching" (Matthew 28:20) process at every point of this journey.

Those involved in formal theological training should partner with those involved in developing disciples. Sunday School and Discipleship Ministries of the Asia-Pacific Region developed a four-fold emphasis that we can use to join our educational institutions and the local church. The goal is "to **exalt** the Lord by helping all people **experience** the saving and transforming work of the Holy Spirit, be **equipped** through the Word of God, be **empowered** for godly service, and **engage** the nations for Christ." This is represented in the following graphic.

**Figure 2:** Asia-Pacific Discipleship Model

This figure merges the being, knowing, and doing of becoming like Jesus. **Experiencing** the saving and transforming work of the Holy Spirit (2 Corinthians 3:18; Ephesians 4:13) brings transformation and renewal into Christ's image (the *being*). **Equipping** comes as disciples add knowledge (*binah* and *yada'*) through training in God's word (the *knowing*) (2 Peter 3:18; 2 Timothy 3:17). **Empowering** happens as believers listen to the Holy Spirit and are guided by godly mentors in service to the world (Romans 12:6) (the *doing*). The result is **engaging** the nations for Christ (1 Corinthians 9:22-23), which will require being, knowing, and doing. At the center of all this is **exalting** God in worship (Romans 12:1-2). People can join this journey at any point.

It is important to emphasize six foundational aspects of this model:

1. *Discipleship is relational.* We have been created by a relational God (Father, Son, and Holy Spirit) to be relational beings (Genesis 1:26-27; 2:18). This is why everything about our faith journey is centered in relationship—first with God and then with others (Matthew 22:37-40). Being a disciple starts as we enter into a relationship with God, with God's church, and with God's world. In other words, we cannot be an effective disciple of Christ in isolation. Being a disciple of Christ is always both communal and personal.

2. *Discipleship is communal and personal.* Discipleship is a "Body" activity rather than an individualistic activity. All believers, not only pastors, are called to be disciples and be actively involved in discipling others. They use their God-given gifts, talents, and resources to

extend God's Kingdom to others through the process of discipleship.

3. ***Discipleship is holistic.*** The five elements of exalting, experiencing, equipping, empowering, and engaging represent a more holistic way of viewing what it means to *be* a disciple and what it means to *do* discipleship. Too often discipleship is relegated to the classroom, becoming only about what we "know." Jesus' call upon his disciples was to "come, follow me" (Mark 1:16). In the process of forming his followers, there was formal teaching, but there was also mentoring and modeling. Jesus lived out his dynamic relationship with the Father before the disciples and inviting them to imitate him. Likewise, our discipleship must be holistic.

4. ***Discipleship is interconnected.*** Within the diagram, the lines between the various elements are intentionally blurred. This is because experiencing, equipping, empowering, and engaging, while each having its own unique aspects, blend together and intersect at multiple points. However, exalting is intentionally placed at the center of the diagram (and first in the definition) because each of the other elements is an act of worship. This interconnected model invites people to enter into the discipleship process at different places (such as worship service, Bible study, service project, and so on).

5. ***Discipleship is inclusive.*** We recognize that God is at the center of who we are and what we are doing; God is our core. No one is truly "outside" the circle of his grace and love. The church needs to meet people where they are and guide them closer to God.

6. ***Discipleship is continuous.*** Discipleship does not have a stopping place. Christians are disciples of Christ for life, and this means they must be continuously involved in the discipleship process—both being discipled and discipling others.

## Transformational Learning

Educators have noted for many years how education brings change to people. More recently, this change has been given the name "transformational learning." The theories behind transformational learning were first developed by Jack Mezirow and have been further developed and expanded by many others. The concept itself is rather simple. People make meaning of their world through their experiences. Most people think and act certain ways without critically analyzing why. Transformational learning seeks to change students by introducing new ideas and values that challenge a person's thinking. This challenge often causes a "disorienting dilemma" that may lead a student to ask new questions and critically reflect on his or her beliefs, assumptions, and values. New ideas and values may lead to a new frame of reference, which may cause some discomfort and tension with old ways of thinking. Mentors can help students navigate this tension and guide the transformation process. Adding knowledge and developing skills will help students navigate new questions and respond to them in healthy ways. This critical reflection develops competence and self-confidence. The result is a changed person who is better equipped for new roles and deeper relationships. The transformed person is then better equipped to participate in the world.

Complexity Theory, then, would suggest that the term "capability" is more of an appropriate goal than "competency" (S. Smith, 42) because of the non-linear circumstances of ministry. That is to say, the context of ministry is always changing, so it is almost impossible to develop a list of tasks or abilities (competencies) that will be adequate. Capability, on the other hand, assumes the ability to adapt a competency for the immediate context to remain effective in ministry. For this reason, in our description of the 4C's, we will substitute *capability* for *competency*.

Transformational learning describes well the desired partnership between discipleship and education. Education provides the opportunity for transformation to take place. It is where being, knowing, and doing are developed through content, capability, character, and context.

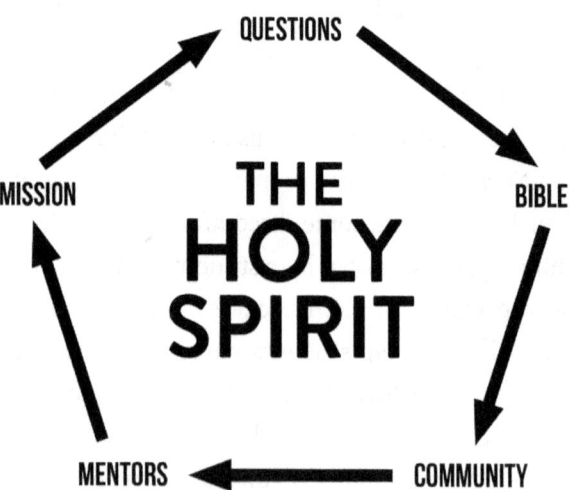

**Figure 3.** Transformational learning is where being, knowing, and doing are developed through content, capability, character, and context.

***Questions*** from various disciplines of study challenge students' presuppositions and world views. Students learn to ask good questions, and it is helpful to provide students a safe place to ask them. However, the questions are not the same each time. As students develop in their understanding, the questions and situations will change. At first, some answers can be provided, but students should gain skill both in asking their own questions and being challenged by the questions of others. Students explore through discovery and discernment, which comprises the content elements within the fields in the bulk of the course. This may also be represented in the advancing courses in the curriculum where content is heavier, and students are learning skills of discernment. Asking questions can also provide students opportunity for spiritual encounters and growth in their faith.

The ***Bible*** provides the primary reference point from which difficult questions can be asked and answered. The Bible may also challenge students' cultures and traditions. Since the Bible is a complex document, skills of interpretation and hermeneutical method are necessary to guide the discovery of new insights. This discovery process will include theological conversation with biblical interpreters of the past and practitioners of the present. This method is termed the Wesleyan Quadrilateral, where tradition, reason, and experience help us interpret God's revelation in the Bible. Teachers help students develop knowledge of the Bible and capability in interpreting and applying it.

Students learn in ***community***. Participatory learning enhances the effectiveness of the environment in which questions are asked and students encounter new ideas and experiences. Growth happens as learners engage in conversation and in times of dissonance as they share ideas and struggles. Organizing education based on cohorts of students enables the learning process to be done in community and to break down the potential isolation that can develop from abstract or academic theological inquiry. Students integrate new theological understandings with personal values. This will lead to the development of new skills. Students are shaped by their encounter with Christ and his community. Disruption and integration through interaction with others can and should also include dialoging with those who do not yet know Jesus, those outside the church. Learning must be seen as part of the mission of making Christlike disciples of all people and not as an end in itself. Students can become engaged in this learning in four areas:

> **With themselves**: Students need to grow in character, understanding, confidence, and skill.
>
> **With other students**: Students learn to function in teams, developing skills in leadership and working with others.
>
> **With a worshipping community**: Being in relation with other believers provides students a dynamic environment to nurture spiritual growth and an opportunity for them to develop skills in working with different people.
>
> **With the larger non-Christian community**: Students learn to listen to those outside the church and interact with diverse people.

Because transformative experiences can be difficult, it is important that students have ***mentors*** to guide them through this process. Since this type of learning requires a critical evaluation of presuppositions and beliefs, it is important that the mentors be available to provide safe places to ask questions and dialogue about possibilities. Teachers should see themselves as mentors through the educational journey of students. They are the primary facilitators for new experiences and awareness through the process of dialogue. Other people can serve as mentors, depending on the topic, place, or purpose of the instruction. Transformative learning can feel threatening and create stress for students. It is risky. So, educators must develop sensitivity to the learners. It is of utmost importance that teachers share the character qualities that match the intended outcomes. Students will learn through imitating what teachers say and how they live. Teaching should be viewed not simply as an educational action but as a spiritual quest whereby Christ's body is being equipped.

The goal of transformational learning *engagement in mission*. Hands-on experiences in real-life settings through the learning process will build skills and confidence in ministry. Transformation takes places as students engage with their cultures and learn from other people. The learning does not end with the completion of a degree program but can continue through lifelong learning. The mentoring does not need to end but may take different shapes with different mentors as students and graduates continue their development. Often the questions asked earlier in the learning process will need to be readdressed as graduates experience new challenges.

This whole process should be **guided by the Holy Spirit**. Transformative learning can be a creative experience whereby a person has new encounters with the Holy Spirit who brings change into the likeness of Christ (2 Corinthians 3:18). Changing our thinking is not enough. We must allow the Holy Spirit to transform us through the means of grace, self-care, and repentance. This transformation takes time, so a careful long-term strategy is required. The result of the education should be character change and more fruitful engagement in the mission of God in the world. The Holy Spirit becomes a participant in personal study times. Choosing to experience change is an act of faith and humility. The Holy Spirit may also speak through the conversations within community and challenge students to grow in wisdom and conviction about their faith.

Old patterns and practices are changing. To be more effective in the mission to which God calls us, we must rethink our models and methods. A new ethos of *teaching* as part of the discipleship process and of *discipling* as part of the educational process must be developed. At the center of this is the character formation of students that leads to effective mission. The highest goal of Christian education is to help students become like Christ and then to live this out through effective engagement in the mission of God. Professional knowledge is important, but students must undergo a fundamental change of outlook that leads to the application of knowledge through loving God and loving neighbor. Character change must lead to mission in the world.

There are several implications of a shift in educational approaches. Fundamentally, there must be a movement from ministry *for education* to *education through ministry*. Learning by doing is essential. This may require keeping students in their context of ministry, which then becomes their classroom. This would require mentoring that focuses on exposing students to new thoughts that challenge their pre-conceptions. Mentors must be creatively developed, with cooperation between teachers, pastors, faculty, or individuals. Pastors should view themselves as teachers and mentors, not only to people within their church, but to other pastors or people who are also in the learning process. Mentors also need to be trained in teaching methodologies, the intended outcomes, and nurtured in their own character formation. Mentoring helps bridge the gap between school and local church and connect students to discipleship.

# CHAPTER THREE

# Transition of Models

Some might say, it is better to strengthen our existing educational models rather than move in a different direction. The following reasons are suggested for the need to re-examine the educational process.

Firstly, one of the strategic priorities of the Asia Pacific Region of the Church of the Nazarene is cohesive education and cohesive ministerial preparation. The vision is to see an educational system where students explore their faith in the local church while maintaining the same educational ethos of a higher education award in one of our educational institutions. We have tended to segment the educational process so that we have a number of parts but little coordination between each part. This regional, strategic priority gives attention to the integration of these various parts. At its best the Church of the Nazarene is an intentional partnership (relationship) between the local church, the District, and the educational system (institution) in a global perspective (Figure 4).

As groups specialize and work in their own area of responsibility, it is possible to disconnect areas that are meant to be in partnership. The tyranny of time pressure, the battle for a fair share of the limited resources, etc. often cause isolation and we become protective of our own patch of ministry responsibility. A process is needed that intentionally works at the cultivation of partnerships between these three aspects of church structure and leadership. Such integration will not simply happen without intention and the implementation of effective strategy.

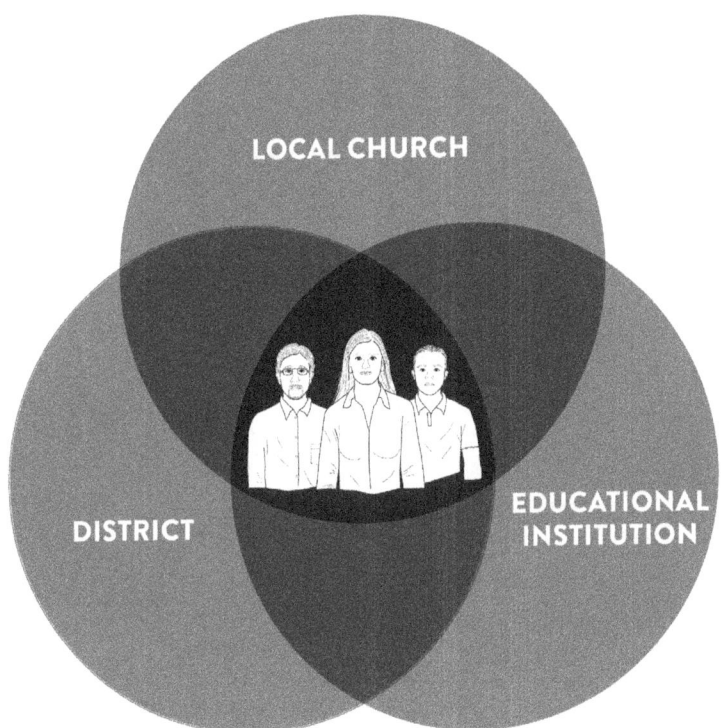

**Figure 4**: A representation of the connection between the local church, district, and the educational system as envisioned by the Church of the Nazarene globally.

There are several ways to conceive of a partnership between the educational institution, the district church, and the local church (see Figure 5).

The Emmaus Model conceives of this partnership in terms of option "C"—interdependence. The benefits of this will be given in the following chapter.

Secondly, a drift away from original purposes (often termed mission drift) is common to most organizations. There is a need to be reminded of our ultimate purposes as the body of Christ and allow these purposes to shape our processes. When these purposes

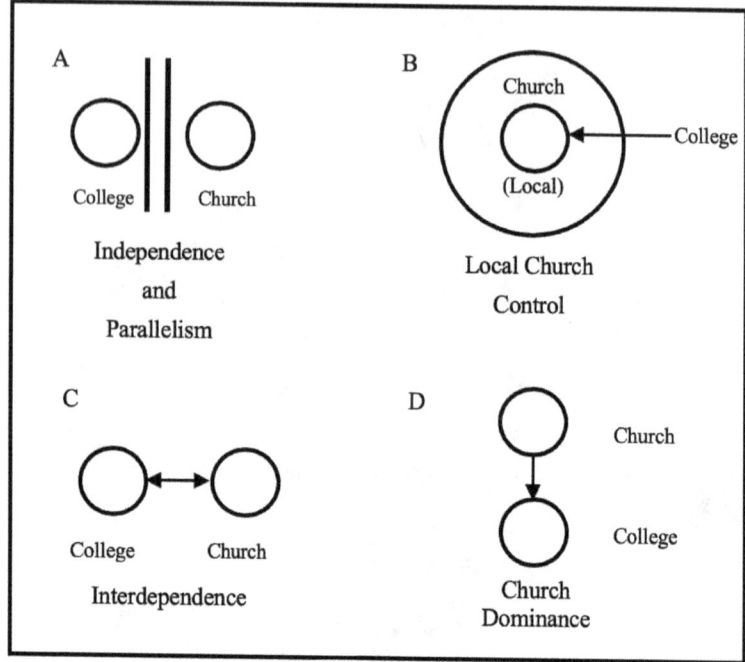

**Figure 5**: Options for conceiving partnership between education and local church (Woodruff, *Toward Excellence in Ministerial Education*, 119).

are clearly established in the core of our identity as a faith community (church) and in all of our structures, there is less likelihood of mission drift. "If you want people to build a ship, don't drum up people to collect wood and don't assign tasks and work, but rather teach them to long for the endless immensity of the sea" (J. Smith, 91). In other words, in keeping the "why" of the educational system constantly before us, there will be a need to periodically adjust our approach.

Thirdly, engaging in specific contexts requires intentional examination of how education is conducted. The environment in which the church is planted will change the final shape of what is grown. The Church of the Nazarene may look very different in

Mongolia compared to Australia, or Japan to Indonesia. However, we pray that the same DNA expresses itself in diverse forms. Working in over 160 world areas demands that the Church of the Nazarene work intentionally with this changing cultural diversity while being guided by the essence of who we are as Nazarenes.

Fourthly, we need to look at our presuppositions to see if they are inappropriately shaping or limiting our horizons of possibility. Making visible the forces that have an impact on us will give us the opportunity to intentionally steer our actions in ways that make us more effective in mission. Presuppositions related to our pedagogies, educational administration, and discipleship all have the potential to limit what can be achieved. If we fail to make these visible or choose not to interact with them can lead to *ad hoc* results and less than robust ways of thinking about solutions.

Fifthly, while the Church of the Nazarene globally has adopted the 4C's as a part of our curriculum design and pedagogy, the urgency for effective mission has led to a pragmatism and competency-based education that lacks the resiliency needed for changing contexts. In other words, we have unintentionally over emphasized competency (capability) at the expense of character formation and context. What is needed for stability in a VUCA world (volatile, uncertain, complex, ambiguous) is to ensure that positive transformation is at the heart of our discipleship. Formation toward Christlikeness is to shape our discipleship, individually and corporately.

Over the 2000 years of Christian education, approaches have been developed that respond to specific contexts at certain times. Even these approaches were contextually driven. With changing contexts, these approaches become increasingly more difficult to apply effectively, and the outcomes may be for a bygone era. The

# THE EMMAUS MODEL

| Symbol | Athens | Berlin | Geneva |
|---|---|---|---|
| Model | Classical | Vocational | Confessional |
| Context | Academy | University | Seminary |
| Goal / Purpose | Transforming the individual | Strengthening the church | Knowing God |
| Emphasis | Personal formation: knowing who... | Interpretive skills: knowing how... | Information, enculturation: knowing what... |
| Formation | Individualized and focused on inner personal, moral, and religious transformation | Clarify vocational identity as the basis for Christian practice | Discursive analysis, comparison and synthesis of beliefs |
| Theology | Theology is the knowledge of God, not about God | Theology is a way of thinking, applying theory to life. Theology is applied: spiritual, missiological, and vocational | Theology is knowing God through a specific tradition |
| Teacher | Provider: of indirect assistance through intellectual and moral disciplines to help students undergo formation | Professor: the teacher is a researcher whom the students assist | Priest: knowledge of tradition, lives and exemplifies it as well as knows it. |
| Student | Cultivates the mind, character and spirit | Becomes a theoretician able to apply practice | Initiated into the tradition, beliefs, vocation and ministry |

**Table 1:** Summary of Models of Theological Education (Das, *Connecting Curriculum*, 17-18)

| Symbol | Jerusalem | Auburn | New Delhi |
|---|---|---|---|
| Model | Missional | Contextual | Spiritual |
| Context | Community | Parish | Ashram |
| Goal / Purpose | Converting the world | Planting locally | Engaging other world views |
| Emphasis | Mission, partnership: knowing for... | Local community: knowhing where... | Multi-cultural, pluralistic: knowing others |
| Formation | Learning has to have refernce to all dimensions of life, family, friendships, work and neighborhood | Learning how to be relevant locally | Learning to co-exist respectully while retainin one's identity |
| Theology | Missiology is the mother of theology. It involved action-mission | Theology is about being spiritually relevant locally | Theology is about understanding the revelation of God in other religious and worldviews |
| Teacher | Practitioner/ Missionary: the teacher is not removed from practice; teaching involves sharing lives as well as truth | Pastor: the teacher leads by being relevant in the community | Apologist: where the teacher not only defends the faith but also builds bridges |
| Student | Discipled to become a disciple-maker | Learns to serve the community | Learns to build bridges and defend the faith |

**Table 1 (continued):** Summary of Models of Theological Education (Das, *Connecting Curriculum*, 17-18)

following is a brief summary of these models, including those developed in more contemporary times.

At first glance the Athens Model appears to hold what we seek to develop—personal character and godliness. However, Banks (p. 20) points out that a fragmentation of theological education occurred with the emergence of universities and the separation of the academic disciplines from each other in the twelfth century. This brought a separation between theory and practice. Education became focused on academic norms and values with a loss of focus on love and moral formation. Theology, once the queen of the sciences, was relegated to a small subset of a much larger discipline of the arts in a university setting.

Subsequent models are best understood as a response to this shifting educational landscape and the inadequacy of the approach to meet the current needs of the church. The Geneva model placed theological education into a confessional context where people were prepared for ministry in a specific theological tradition. The tendency with this kind of model is to become insular and inward looking—the very opposite of what we want to see in effective mission. In these models, mission effectiveness was the presumed outcome. However, Banks (p. 157f) intentionally places mission back into the heart of the theological education enterprise.

This missional approach places involvement in ministry at the heart of the educational enterprise with reflection and reflective practice the pedagogy of learning. One of the difficulties with an educational process away from the practice of that learning, is the creation of a theory and practice division (sometimes described as a barrier) that can leave a learner well equipped with theory but having little ability to apply that theory. By bringing action into the heart of the learning process, this artificially created barrier is removed. However, effective learning takes place when there is *reflective* practice, not just practice. This is where the Banks' approach can fail, not because of an inherent problem with his model, but because of ineffective reflective practice. The reflection that is needed is neither an abstract thinking about action nor is it simply a pragmatic response to concrete situations. Banks suggests five key questions in effective reflective practice:

1. What kind of world do we live in?
2. What should we do?
3. What are the basic needs, tendencies, and values we should satisfy?
4. What constraints does our present cultural, sociological, or ecological context place on our actions?
5. What are the concrete rules and roles we should follow?

After we have asked these questions and begun to build a solid descriptive theological understanding of the situation, we can explore what the Bible and the Christian tradition have to offer.... It is important that [we] "act out," not just "learn from" the educational process (Banks, 160).

This approach resonates with many evangelical traditions (including the Church of the Nazarene) where the making of disciples is a passionate focus. This, though, has been its downfall. In our impatience to be on mission, there is a tendency toward pragmatic action with its visible, measurable results. The nuanced reflective action that is so much a part of the Banks model has been overlooked (Austin and Perry 2015). The result has been a minimal focus on character formation and an over-emphasis on unreflective action. The consequences of such a trend is toward moral failures of leaders, inflexible ministry processes that focus on the method and mechanisms rather than people, a ministry that is equipped for a context that is no longer relevant, and a loss of life-giving vision, to name just a few.

The following Emmaus Model seeks to synthesize Banks' missional model and the Athens classical model. However, the Emmaus Model brings the mission and the Christlike character formation together and makes both the focus of theological education. When this is done, we would see that "theological education is not a higher stage of Christian education, but a dimension of everyone's Christian education, depending upon their stage in life and calling" (Banks p. 157). In summary then, the Emmaus Model includes the following:

1. Character formation at the core of the educational process
2. A missional perspective throughout which embraces both passion (heart) and skills (head)
3. Inclusive of lay and clergy
4. A spiritual dynamic that is empowered by God's Spirit and has a strong experiential component
5. Sustainability that is in terms of reproducibility.

# CHAPTER FOUR

# The Emmaus Journey

## Introduction

In Luke 24:13-25 we have an illustration of transformational learning. The change that took place in the two disciples on that first Easter Sunday is remarkable. Initially they were confused, disappointed, and not sure what to think about the circumstances that had taken place around them. They had witnessed Jesus' crucifixion. That didn't fit their expectations of the Messiah! Then they heard rumors of Jesus' resurrection. That was completely outside of their world view! This was the context for their walk back to their home village, Emmaus.

The features that created the opportunity for transformative learning included what may be thought of as negative—confusion and disarray. However, "Jesus himself came up and walked along with them" (Luke 24:15b). This turned the negative into a positive. As Jesus took the time to walk with them and hear them express their confusion and disappointment, he was able to provide a perspective that brought understanding. "And beginning with Moses and all the Prophets, he explained to them what was said in all the Scriptures concerning himself" (Luke 24:27).

It is important to note that this is not where the learning stopped. In fact, this is really the prelude to the major learning that would take place. The insight from the Scripture formed the foundation, or to use another analogy, the scaffold, on which life change was to take place. Once hospitality was extended to Jesus, the disciples gathered around the meal table. Note the highly relational connection Jesus made with these two confused disciples. It was while Jesus was breaking bread that a flash of insight and recognition came to the disciples. This was Jesus, the resurrected Christ! What followed next was truly transformational. Jesus disappeared, but the disciples began to talk with each other about this experience which led to a new passion for following the Messiah! "Were not our hearts burning within us while he talked with us on the road and opened the Scriptures to us?" (Luke 24:32)

The transformation was evident in these confused and discouraged disciples, who rushed back to Jerusalem with no regard for their personal safety, to proclaim, "We have seen the risen Christ!" Confusion was replaced with assurance, timidity with courage, and sadness with joy! Now that was a transformation!

With this as background the following approach to learning is called the "Emmaus Model" (see Figure 6).

## The Model Explained

There are several components that go into this model that require specific definition. Firstly, as described in Chapter 2

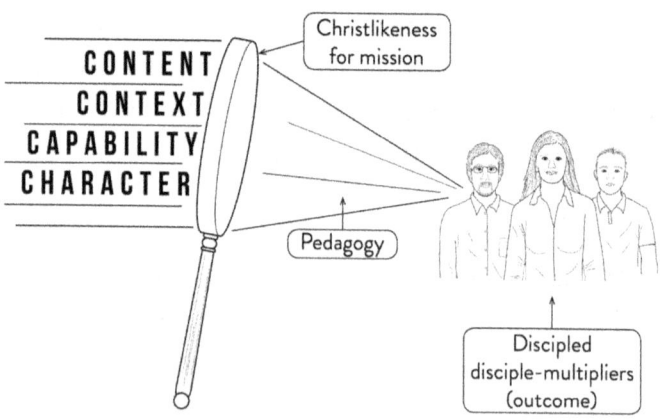

**Figure 6.** The Emmaus Model

(Education in the Nazarene Perspective), there are at least 4 components that are involved in the process of theological education: content, context, capability, and character (the 4C's). It is difficult to embrace all four components in a balanced way that leads to transformation. Instead, an overemphasis on content makes the student knowledgeable but not necessarily effective in the practice of ministry. An undue focus on context can result in an educational process that lacks coherency as we react to various world views, cultures and interpretations of Scripture. Keeping capability the primary focus leaves us simply doing a job that can lack an ethical dimension or a passion for the work. A focus on character alone can leave us unable to practically apply insights in intellectually robust ways in situations that are forever changing.

The critical component in addressing a balance in the 4C's is the "lens" through which the 4C's pass. This "lens" will give coherence to the curriculum. However, in our model the lens has become a magnifying glass rather than a prism. We determine our desired outcomes by examining what an effective discipled discipler looks like. This examination, then, helps us understand the characteristics we want to see in a graduate of our pastoral formation process. We use the magnifying glass as a means of focussing the 4C's on those we disciple. Ultimately, the purpose of our educational program is to meet the needs of our mission and the needs of our churches in this mission. This cannot be over-emphasized! If we are not intentional about this, we may become mired in the detail of an educational program that may create wonderful learning but lose the purpose of this learning.

The Great Commission (Matthew 28:19-20) and the Great Commandment (Matthew 22:34-40) express what we need as the outcome in this educational process. We want a graduate of this process to be a loving disciple of Christ who makes Christlike disciples who in turn make Christlike disciples. To be in mission requires our graduates to be disciple makers, not just better disciples. The vision of our educational program is to have students multiplying disciples as a way of life, and that their journey of being disciples of Christ is becoming richer and deeper along the way.

Even this may be too small a focus. Das explains using "program logic" for a "theological institution" in Figure 7. Educational systems tend to focus on the output level but there is a need to focus on the outcome level. When measuring the outcome for educational systems effectiveness, we look at the graduates' effectiveness in the missional church. Hence, the focus is a discipled disciple-multiplier. If we keep this outcome in sharp focus, we can then track backward to explore what features are needed in our educational system to obtain this outcome.

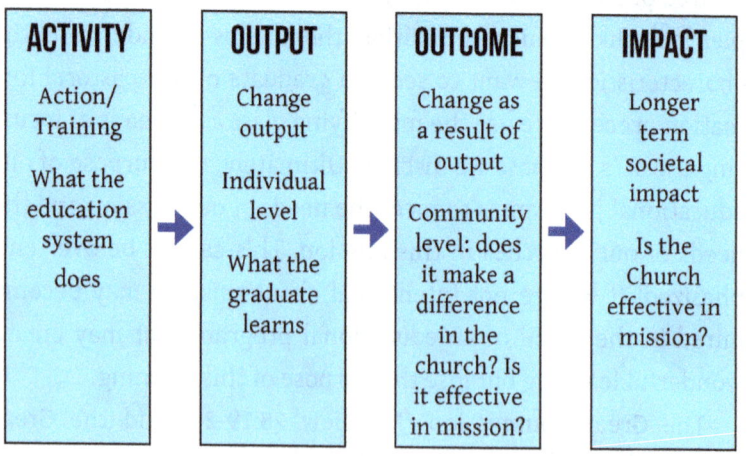

**Figure 7:** A program logic chain (adapted from Das, p. 46 "Connecting Curriculum and Context" in *Is It Working?*

Now that we have described the outcome we desire from the educational system, we can now ask the question, What lens do we need to bring the 4C's into focus toward that end? The Emmaus Model suggests "Christlikeness for, and in, mission" as that lens. This brings together the lenses of the *classical* (personal formation) and *missional* (making disciples) models of theological education in a synergistic way. Table 2 gives a comparison of the two models that the Emmaus Model synthesizes and the resultant features of the Emmaus Model.

In the Emmaus Model there are at least two dimensions at work in the lens.

1. **Christlikeness**. By Christlikeness we mean authentic being, positive character formation, and living as a genuine Christ-follower. Starting the journey with Christ means that there is someone new in our lives, and our identity is in Christ (2 Corinthians 5:17). This is not a static state of being, but rather entrance into a new relationship with God. In this new relationship, we learn how to love and how to fulfil our original calling as humans to be in loving union with God (John 17:21-22). Discipleship explores this relationship and is a journey into a deeper and more meaningful relational connection with God in Christ through the Holy Spirit. There is a tangible and practical dimension to this because this exploration is done in the context of a community. The lens requires an emphasis on formation and spiritual nurture and a safe relational place in which to process content, experiences and probing questions.

2. **Mission**. This is the context in which character formation occurs. The formation is not just about becoming an

# THE EMMAUS MODEL

| Symbol | Athens | Jerusalem | Emmaus |
|---|---|---|---|
| **Model** | Classical | Missional | Journey in the company of others |
| **Context** | Academy | Community | Community of faith living in the wider diverse world |
| **Goal/ Purpose** | Transforming the individual | Converting the world | Discipled 'disciple-multiplier' as a lifelong learner |
| **Emphasis** | Personal formation: knowing who ... | Mission, partnership: knowing for ... | Personal and group formation toward Christlikeness in the *missio Dei* |
| **Formation** | Individualized and focused on inner personal, moral and religious transformation | Learning has to have reference to all dimensions of life, family, friendships, work and neighborhood | Shaped by encounter with Christ and His community |
| **Theology** | Theology is the knowledge of God, not about God | Missiology is the mother of theology. It involves action - mission. | A theology of embodiment of the Gospel i.e. Incarnation of Kingdom of God principles and servanthood |
| **Teacher** | Provider: of indirect assistance through intellectual and moral disciplines to help students undergo formation | Practitioner/ missionary: the teacher is not removed from practice; teaching involves sharing lives as well as truth | Discipler/Mentor/ Coach/fellow-learner sharing life as well as knowledge |
| **Student** | Cultivates the mind, character and spirit | Discipled to become a disciple-maker | Discipled to be a disciple-maker and shaper of culture |

**Table 2:** Comparison of the Athens, Jerusalem and Emmaus models (adapted from Das *Connecting Curriculum with Context*, p. 17)

ethical, well rounded person in the Kingdom of God. It is about fulfilling our God-given vocation to be involved in the *missio Dei*. Christlikeness is not an end in itself. It is the means by which we are engaged in the *mission Dei*. In other words, the shaping and forming toward Christlikeness happens **while** we are involved in the mission of God. The Emmaus Model is not about preparing people for the mission and then going and doing the mission. It is about learning as we are doing the mission, i.e. Christlikeness for and in God's mission in his world.

If these two dimensions become the lens through which the 4C's pass, then our pedagogy and our educational processes may be different to what we have been accustomed. This is student centered, mission-focused, and a means toward a much bigger goal than simply mastering biblical and theological content. This approach requires us to capture the grandeur of the ends of this education, and not just focus on the means. The thrill of seeking the kingdom of God and that is seeking understanding from a faith position, puts us in a position for transformative theological education. The implications for teaching and learning are developed further in the next chapter.

# CHAPTER FIVE

# Implementing the Model

How we teach and how we respond in teaching moments with students will reveal what we really believe. All pedagogy assumes a certain understanding of humanity and personhood. While this is not the place to explore this in depth, one important assumption in this model is that the created order carries within it a purpose given to it by a purposeful Creator. Truth, beauty, and goodness are discovered, and learning is approached through a humble, listening posture (Messmore, p. 40).

Smith says, "Education in virtue is not like learning the Ten Commandments. Education in virtue is a kind of formation, a retraining of our dispositions. Learning isn't just information acquisition; it is more like inscribing something into the very fibre of your being.... We learn virtues through imitation" (J. Smith, pp. 16-20). It is to this emphasis that the Emmaus Model attempts to be faithful. The implications for this kind of learning and teaching are profound. A few are considered very briefly.

## Ministry Formation is more than a "Hoop to Jump Through"

With the desire to reach the very significant event of ordination in the Church of the Nazarene, one can be tempted to think of this as a goal. Rather, it is the next door through which to pass in our calling and our discipleship. We learn a way of living and a perspective on life that carries us into and through the formal educational process. Our learning develops our understanding of *who* we are as much as it is about being equipped for service. The process commences as a disciple in the local faith fellowship (local church) and continues into the academy and then beyond. This is not theoretical ruminations on esoteric ideas, but a practical and livable reshaping of our priorities and passions in the light of the Gospel. Transformation of the individual and of the communities in which the student ministers is the expected outcome. This is a big vision!

However, there is an assumption that underlies this: that the disciple (student and teacher) is active in the mission of making Christlike disciples. In this model, one does not retire to a place out of ministry and service in order to learn to be equipped. The disciple is learning on-the-job, however ill-equipped the student may feel at the time. Much like the disciples on the Emmaus road in the Gospel of Luke, their hearts "burned within them" as Jesus explained the Scriptures to them. From that, they burned with a passion to share the good news with the other disciples. Their behavior changed as a result of their meaningful encounter with Jesus and the Scriptures. Ultimately discipleship becomes more about story than static concepts, more about the dynamic of relationships than about cognitive prowess.

## The Student—Teacher Encounter

The encounter between student and teacher is a safe place for exploration and the processing of content as it relates to living in the mission of God. The teacher is a mentor and "playing coach" rather than simply a content specialist who has a focus on development and delivery of that content. Often, the teacher and student discover new things together and create new perspectives out of their encounter with each other and their context. This is highly relational. As teachers we follow the Apostle Paul's admonition, "Be imitators of me, as I am of Christ" (1 Corinthians 11:1).

This relationship is cultivated as a safe place to work through difficult questions that challenge personal values, world-view differences, and dissonance. Care, love, and an unwavering commitment to seek the best for the student is at the heart of this. Instilling confidence in the student to press ahead in growing and being an encourager reflects this kind of commitment.

The ethos of the classroom, which may be any place students gather, influences the type and extent of the learning that can take place. For example, the teacher needs to model a dependency on God through praying before each formal class session, asking for a student's reflection on their past week and their encounter with someone in the community, or reading Scripture and the teacher giving testimony to the learning through that reading. There are many other practical examples that give expression to the activity of the classroom modelling an openness to hear from God, and a safe place to question and probe difficulties. After all, this is a journey together, and habits such as these are formational. Students can discern what we truly believe as teachers by what we do in the classroom.

> You yourselves are our letter, written on our hearts, known and read by everyone. You show that you are a letter from Christ, the result of our ministry, written not with ink but with the Spirit of the living God, not on tablets of stone but on tablets of human hearts (2 Corinthians 3:2-3).

The teacher as mentor and playing coach can assist in engaging the student in the "zone of proximal development." This is the synergy that comes in the student-teacher relationship which allows the student to extend his or her understanding into areas that can only be reached with help. The more experienced teacher or the content specialist (the knowledgeable other) can come alongside students and stretch their capabilities into new areas of knowledge.

One of the challenges we face in this student—teacher relationship is technology. On-line learning and video conferencing are our new reality. To ensure accessibility, not all students will be present physically in a traditional classroom. There are many studies that purport to show that on-line learning can be relational. It is not our intention to debate this here, but rather to acknowledge we need to find a way to engage relationally so that interactions are rich and vibrant, not static. Developing cohorts of students, requiring face to face facilitation at times, requiring engagement in on-line conversations with class members, are just a few ways that relationships might be cultivated. The Emmaus Model requires such relationships as an essential element in the educational process. This means that "self-studies" and "directed studies" must include avenues for relational connections. This will almost certainly require us to retool our current practice.

## The Arena for Learning

Students' life of discipleship in the wider community is the context in which learning takes place. One of the advantages of this is that the theory–practice divide is minimized. Traditionally we learn in a theoretical fashion away from the practice of ministry. We then wonder how to apply that theory. This model requires the student to ask questions of the context in which they live and work. The students seek knowledge to work through perceived issues. When confronted with practical needs and questions, the motivation of the students to learn is rarely a problem. The resultant integration can provide a robust educational outcome. This does not mean that the students are simply reactive to the experiences. There will be times that the case is made for proactive preparation, in the light of previous experience. Nevertheless, it will be learning on the job.

With this model there is no need to extract the student from the ministry context. In the past students who have had to withdraw from their ministry context for further theological education have been hampered by costs, adjusting to new surroundings that have sometimes not been hospitable, and difficulties in finding a place of service when returning home. The fact that the local ministry setting has to be without key leaders while the student is away in education, has also hindered the church. Keeping the arena for education in a student's context has many benefits.

Another assumption that is made in this model is that learning will take place within a community of disciples. One way is by being embedded in the faith fellowship while learning. Additionally, it may be possible to have a formal cohort of fellow students from a variety of ministry settings journey together. In Fowler's developmental view of faith formation, there are key moments of confusion and dissonance that inevitably come the way of all who are deepening in faith. In fact, education can create those moments of dissonance. Keeping such experiences and education in the crucible of relationships helps prevent the loss of faith that can so often accompany this dissonance. This is discipling one another.

## The Place of Theological Reflection

At the core of the pedagogy in the Emmaus Model is reflective practice. This requires the ability to reflect theologically on ministry experience, discerning the activity of the Holy Spirit and learning from that activity. It also assumes that there is a deepening knowledge of the Scripture. The reflection does not take place in a vacuum. Experience is drawn into the light of Scripture, and the Holy Spirit helps, guides and shapes us in the midst of that experience (John 16:13-14). Reflective practice, though, requires the learning to include action. Decisions are made, actions initiated, and change takes place. Action and reflection are two phases of the same process.

It must be stressed that such reflection is not just the activity of a trained clergy. This is something that all disciples can and must do. It is an ongoing conversation about God at work, and this conversation has been going on through the ages. It is a demanding task because it allows for the appreciation of diversity, healthy debate and creative tension. There can be an open-endedness that can feel uncomfortable or unresolved. This is what keeps us dependent upon the Holy Spirit and the community of faith to bring wisdom. It is the opportunity to exhibit the fruits of the Spirit (Galatians 5:22-26).

When dealing with a specific situation from which we can learn, the following questions are helpful:

1. Who is involved in this situation and what are the circumstances?
2. Where is God in this situation? What are some of the underlying theological themes?
3. What are my own assumptions in this situation? Does my understanding of who God is need to be challenged?
4. What questions arise from this?
5. What can be my response to this situation? How can I change? What can I do as a consequence?

## Transformative Education Takes Time

The Emmaus Model of theological education relies heavily on a relational connection between student, teacher and the insight gained for its formative aspects. This means that this process cannot be rushed. If the model focussed merely on content, then 24 courses for ordination could be delivered in 24 weekend intensives. However, this is not what the global Church of the Nazarene needs; hence the prescription that these studies need to be completed over the *equivalent of three years full time study*. Messmore (p. 47) says that many teachers seem to place a confidence and devotion in the science of knowledge (including the analysis of Scripture) in the realm of neutral instruments for utilitarian purposes. However, a relational epistemology suggests that knowing is a relationship between the knower and the known. This sparks curiosity and delight, discovery and joy. There is a need to live in that relationship, and not rush too quickly into the mechanics of yet another 'concept' to be applied. "Reflection worthy of practical theologians is theologically rich in character rather than the poor cousins of psychology or contextual analysis" (Patterson p 11).

Transformative education will deal with issues at the heart of our world view. There will be challenges of previously strongly held opinions. Questions will arise and uncertainty will emerge amid confusing times. Without the safety of caring, thoughtful, educative relationships, there is the temptation to brush these questions aside or to be satisfied with glib answers that will not deal with reality. This process can't be rushed. While the need to equip pastors and leaders is urgent, we dare not short cut the transformative element to theological education. The good news is that students (disciples) can be in ministry while in the formal educational process. This is strongly encouraged as the preferred context for theological education. As such this is not an 'either / or' situation—either 'ministry or education'. It is a 'both / and' situation! Let's not be tempted to ignore one over the other for the sake of having a person fill a leadership role.

## Assessing the Curriculum

Assessment seeks to clarify the level of impact on the student, the educational system and the local church. It is a tool of evaluation that is done at various milestones on the journey. Without such moments of assessment, judgement on effectiveness can be left to what is immediately in front of us. There are several challenges to assessment in the Emmaus Model.

Firstly, we can shift the focus of what we assess from what is done in the classroom to the impact students have in their context. Cunningham (p. 29) gives an example of assessing a program on clean water. We could measure how many classes were taught on teaching the importance of clean water. We could measure how many demonstrations of boiling water were conducted, or we could assess how the fall in infant mortality rate as a consequence of mothers learning and actually boiling the water to kill germs. Obviously, we are wanting to measure the impact or the outcome rather than the input. This becomes a little more difficult when we start looking at formation and disciple making. However, our curriculum can be shaped to keep impact in mind, and this is where we need to give our attention. It is much easier to measure inputs. Even with outcomes-based education, we easily fall into the temptation of measuring outputs that have little effect on impact.

As we assess our curriculum, it is important to reassert that theological education is not an end in itself. Theological education is meant to serve the church. Our strength comes as we partner between education provider, district, and local church.

Whenever one of these partnerships breaks or becomes strained, to that extent we have an ineffective educational system because:

1. It is difficult to effectively measure impact and then adjust curriculum.
2. It is difficult to keep students in context for their education.

It is imperative that nurturing the relationships between education provider, district, and local church be an intentional and regular focus.

This leads to a second challenge. Relationships are vital in the Emmaus Model. However, these relationships are involved at different levels creating a diversity of engagement. For example, Table 3 means to show the inclusive nature of this educational process that results in complexity.

Despite the diversity, there is a unity found in the commitment to spiritual and character formation (identified in the lens as growing in Christlikeness) and a common focus toward a discipled discipler. Our assessments may be identifying smaller steps on the journey, the assessment tasks should not distract from the impact we seek.

A third challenge in assessment is dealing with practical contexts. While we do not want to limit the assessment to a 'tick the box' ability statement or review, we do want to see that the formation and transformation that takes place within a practical ministry context is identified and acknowledged. The Emmaus Model seeks intentional life change and character formation that is not left to chance or osmosis. Assessing such change has always been a challenge in an educational setting. We will need to think through clearly the formation indicators, develop those indicators and collect information on these for formative assessment (Hockridge p. 336).

These are just a few of the larger implications of this model. As the model is applied, many practical issues will emerge that will require focused conversation. This is, after all, a dynamic and growing model.

# THE EMMAUS MODEL

|  | Key Questions | Theology Training for Laity | Theology Training for Christians in the Marketplace, professions etc. |
|---|---|---|---|
| Target / Focus | Who is the target? | Local faith community; new Christians | Professionals who sense a call to be in the work place as their ministry |
| Main Content | What is the content of the training? | Spiritual and character formation. Understanding the faith community and its place within the wider community. | Spiritual and character formation. Understanding the faith community and its place in the community; the nature of being a culture maker and culture shaper. |
| Purpose | Why is this training being done? | To disciple and be a disciple-maker / multiplier | To be a disciple-maker / multiplier and reflective practitioner |
| Method | How is this training to be done? | Small groups at congregational level; learning by doing in mission; short term classes | Small groups (formal cohorts); seminars; workshops |
| Ethos | What values and spirituality permeate the training? | Growing together toward Christlikeness in mission | Growing together toward Christlikeness; spiritual discernment |
| Context | Where is the training conducted? | Homes and local faith communities | Homes, local churches, workplace |
| People | Who. How does the faith of those involved define the education? | Members of the community of faith | Members of the community of faith involved in the market place; pastors; leaders |

**Table 3.** The inclusive, complex nature of the Emmaus Model

## IMPLEMENTING THE MODEL

| *Training for Ministerial Theology* | *Training for Professional Theology* | *Training for Academic Theology* |
|---|---|---|
| Lay Leadership in local faith communities | Clergy / Leadership | Teachers of clergy and researchers |
| Spiritual and character formation. Christian leadership, hermeneutics and understanding the faith community and its place within the wider community. | Spiritual and character formation. Biblical studies; theology; theological reflection; critical thinking; | Spiritual and character formation. Research skills; theological reflection; discernment; critical thinking. |
| Equip for service as a disciple-multiplier and equip others as reflective practitioner | Equipping others for ministry as disciple-multipliers; specialist ministry and study | Equipping others as disciple-multipliers; specialist studies |
| Small groups (formal cohorts); seminars; workshops. | Learning cohorts in ministry contexts | Academy |
| Growing together toward Christlikeness; spiritual discernment | Growing together toward Christlikeness, discovery; spiritual discernment; community of faith formation | Growing together toward Christlikeness; critical thinking and inquiry |
| Local faith communities; academy; faith community networks | Local faith communities; academy; faith communities networks | Local faith communities; academy |
| Some members of the community of faith; leaders | Pastors and leaders / mentors | Pastors and leaders / mentors |

# CONCLUSION

The mission to which God has called us is to make disciples. This is the mission for all Christians at all levels of the church, from local faith communities to the academy. As cultures and contexts change and the mission of God expands, we must think of new ways to be effective in mission. The development of the Emmaus model is a work in progress. The current form is the result of conversations with educators and ministry practitioners over the last three years. As the conversation continues there will be adjustments and changing perspectives that will hopefully strengthen the model.

The model builds on the past and brings together character formation toward Christlikeness and a passionate engagement in mission. Each of the 4C's is important and must be nurtured in the discipleship journey.

- Content provides the foundation and scaffolding for learning and helps students connect thinking and learning to the world around them.
- Context gives the laboratory for asking questions and the place where mission is carried out.
- Capability increases as skills grow through learning content, experiencing personal change, and becoming more self-aware of one's place in God's mission.
- Character develops as students engage with each other, teachers, and mentors through the spiritual disciplines with a growing awareness of God's activity in His world.

The Emmaus Model is highly relational in its orientation as students learn together and are guided by experienced and passionate mentors who are themselves engaged in the mission of making disciples. As such the model affirms:

- All are called into ministry wherever Christians find themselves and need to be equipped for that ministry.
- Theological education is about developing Christlike character in mission and doing this within a faith community.
- This education begins in the local church with intentional discipleship.
- The educational process is a shared responsibility between educators, the local church, the mentors, and district boards.
- Teachers have a catalytic role in the development of discipled disciplers maturing in Christlikeness.
- Learning takes place in the crucible of doing ministry.
- The educational process is a lifelong pursuit not just restricted to its formal elements.

To effectively engage this model, there is a need to intentionally draw college boards, administrators, and faculty members into the task of transformation and mission. The Wesleyan-Holiness theological tradition is beautifully positioned to express the relational and transformational elements of making Christlike disciples of the nations. Embracing a genuine partnership with the local church, the District, and the academy helps us to respond to the uniqueness of each context. We can stay nimble and effective in the midst of diversity. Clearly, there is strength in doing this together. In this shared responsibility, the journey is surprisingly simple, but it is not easy. We need God's Spirit to transform us, empower us, and work through us.

I pray that out of his glorious riches he may strengthen you with power through his Spirit in your inner being, so that Christ may dwell in your hearts through faith. And I pray that you, being rooted and established in love, may have power, together with all the Lord's holy people, to grasp how wide and long and high and deep is the love of Christ, and to know this love that surpasses knowledge—that you may be filled to the measure of all the fullness of God (Ephesians 3:16-19).

# BIBLIOGRAPHY

Austin, Denise A. Perry, David. "From Jerusalem to Athens: A Journey of Pentecostal Pedagogy in Australia." *Journal of Adult Theological Education Education* 12, no. 1 (May 2015): 43-55.

Banks, Robert. *Reenvisioning Theological Education: Exploring a Missional Alternative to Current Models.* Grand Rapids: Eerdmans, 1999.

Board of General Superintendents. *Nazarene Essentials. Church of the Nazarene, 2015.* Retrieved from http://nazarene.org/sites/default/files/essentials/docs/NazareneEssentials1.2.pdf.

Cunningham, Scott. "Assessment Beyond the 4Bs." In *Is it Working? Researching Context to Improve Curriculum*, edited by Stuart Brooking. Carlisle, Cumbria, UK: Langham Global Library, 2018.

Das, Rupen. *Connecting Curriculum with Context.* Carlisle, Cumbria, UK: Langham Global Library, 2015, 17-18. Adapted from Brian Edgar, "The Theology of Theological Education," *Evangelical Review of Theology* 29, no. 3 (2005): 208-17.

Fowler, James. *Faith Development and Pastoral Care.* Philadelphia, PA: Fortress Press, 1986.

Hockridge, Diane. "Reimagining Christian Formation in Online Theological Education. In *Reimagining Christian Education: cultivating transformative approaches*, edited by Johannes M. Luetz, Tony Dowden, and Beverley Norsworthy. Singapore: Springer, 2018.

Louw, Mark L. "Character Formation Through Theological Education in Community." Unpublished dissertation in partial fulfillment of Master of Arts in Theology, Nazarene Theological College, Manchester, May, 2012.

Messmore, Ryan. "The Trinity, Love and Higher Education: Recovering Communities of Enchanted Learning." In *Reimagining Christian Education: Cultivating Transformative Approaches*, edited by Johannes M. Luetz, Tony Dowden, Beverley Norsworthy. Singapore: Springer, 2018.

Mezirow, J. (1978). "Perspective Transformation." *Adult Education Quarterly Adult Education Quarterly* 28, no. 2 (1978): 100-110.

Paterson, Michael. "Discipled by praxis: soul and role in context." *Practical Theology* 12, no. 1 (2019: 7-19.

Smith, James K.A. *You Are What You Love: The Spiritual Power of Habit.* Grand Rapids: Brazos Press, 2016.

Smith, Stephen. "Moving from Instruction to Inquiry: How Complexity Theory Informs Work-Integrated Learning." In *Wondering About God Together*, edited by Les Ball and Peter Bolt. Sydney, Australia: SCD Press, 2018.

Tibi, Stéphane. Eurasia Regional Education Coordinator, Church of the Nazarene.

Woodruff, Robert L. *Education on Purpose: Models for Education in World Areas.* QUT Publications, 2001.

Woodruff, Robert L. "Towards Excellence in Ministerial Education: An Educational Model for Program Development and Improvement." St. Mark's National Theological Centre, Canberra, Australia, 1993.

www.ingramcontent.com/pod-product-compliance
Lightning Source LLC
Chambersburg PA
CBHW071315060426
42444CB00036B/3056